POETRY

from the

HISTORY

of

POLITICS, SOCIETY, CULTURE

and

CLIMATE CHANGE

A Poet's-Eye View of the
Last Twelve Decades 1900 to 2020

"poetry bares the dirt, the deceit....the avarice
and the angst, just as it bursts asunder
fragrant, febrile, feelings.... of love, and lust?"

from: *"The Poet and our Planet"*

Peter Fernandez

ISBN: 978-1-8382501-0-2 (Paperback)
ISBN: 978-1-8382501-1-9 (Kindle 'Print Replica' eBook)

Contents

Acknowledgements

I wish to thank:

My wife Marina and son Alex for their patience while I was immersed in the research of events, collection of statistics, and creation of this collection;

Liz Berry, Caroline Bird, Rishi Dastidar, Gregory Leadbetter, Jo Bell, Peter Kahn, Sasha Dugdale, Kathryn Maris, Claudia Rankine, Moniza Alvi, Rebecca Watts, Katherine Lockton, Kei Miller, Jane Commane and Jericho Brown, whose incisive suggestions and perceptive advice influenced some of the poems;

Glyn Maxwell, Emily Berry, Beth Davyson, Paul McGrane, Hannah Lowe, Rory Waterman and Mona Arshi. Their valuable reviews, articles, essays and poetry are gems. I must confess, I keep dipping into their wealth of poetry nuggets from time to time.

Introduction

"There is not a particle of life which does not bear poetry within it"

– Gustave Flaubert

"The past itself is not a narrative. In its entirety, it is as chaotic, uncoordinated, and complex as life. History is about making sense of that mess, finding or creating patterns and meanings and stories from the maelstrom."

– John H. Arnold

Today, with demands on our time coming at us from all sides, we simply cannot wade through thick tomes of thousands of pages of a history book or two, to appreciate the key milestones that brought us to our present here-and-now. I have curated relevant historic events and people connected with them, to extract the poetry within. As Aristotle pointed out "Poetry is finer and more philosophical than history, for poetry expresses the universal, and history only the particular".

The fact that most of us only have a vague idea of the major events in history that have significantly altered the course of global politics, societies, cultures and climate, inspired me to write "Poetry from the History of Politics, Society, Culture and Climate Change" from 1900 to 2020.

In absolute terms, while the facts of events are immutable, their narratives presented by historians are not. They are frequently distorted by individual agendas of apologists, revisionists, nationalists and other special interest groups. I have also explored the historiography rather than just the history of the events, to probe the subtle, and not so subtle, distortions.

For the reader to grasp the consequences of the major events, the choice of the period was deliberate, as our present way of life has, to a large extent, been influenced by the continuum of twists and turns of events of the last twelve decades. The only exception is the poem about the British Empire which required the backstory of how a trading company, The British East India Company (BEIC), virtually established itself as a country within a country until the

British Government decided to abolish it altogether after the Indian Rebellion of 1857, and India soon became the jewel in the crown of the British Empire.

World Wars and other conflicts, between and within nations, played significant roles in shaping our present world. While these events play out in short periods of time, the consequences of most conflicts linger for decades, perhaps centuries, hence the inclusion of poems about relevant wars and conflicts was essential to provide the distilled truth that usually lurks somewhere in the thousands of pages of history books. In the words of William Wordsworth, "Poetry is the spontaneous overflow of powerful feelings: it takes its origin from emotion recollected in tranquility." Looking back on the period, I was moved by the display of courage, passion and selfless drive of certain individuals whose actions and perseverance to achieve their honourable objectives were nothing short of inspiring. Starkly opposing these admirable qualities, were those of other individuals who were equally bent on destroying lives, committing murder and mayhem and the vilest deeds against people and places. The spectrum of emotions running through me while researching both these types of individuals compelled me to probe their lives and the words just spat onto the screen as my fingertips frantically trod the keyboard.

I have given readers, where required, some expositions in the form of contextual notes of the time frame in which a poem is embedded, so that one can relate and appreciate the lingering nuances of the word and our world as we traversed through these decades.

As this collection of poems is about historic events, its remit by definition had to be confined to providing clarity in the poems to convey the underlying message, with disciplined dial-tweaks between poetic flights of fancy and down-to-earth descriptions of facts.

The poems are a fair mix of free-verse, sonnets, and blends of contemporary styles of the decades, with universality to resonate and reveal the heart of the message while avoiding the pitfall of over-intellectualising its rib cage. Leaving space for the reader to breathe the essence of the poem within the lines.

Cultures through art, science, philosophy, religion and literature are always introducing norms into societies—— both prescriptive and proscriptive. Ultimately, culture defines a society by the norms that it adopts, adapts and assimilates.

Since Enheduanna of Mesopotamia

I start this collection with a poem that displays the funny-at-times/screwed-up-at-times rivalry that has existed in varying forms, in the realm of poetry. Largely, the rivalry has enabled informative debates and helped keep poetry fresh and relevant in academia without alienating or excluding the general reader completely.

The Akkadian poet **Enheduanna** (2285-2250 BCE) was a princess, priestess, and poet in Ancient Mesopotamia which today comprises Iraq and Kuwait. It has the enviable reputation of being the cradle of civilisation. At its southernmost is the region of Sumer.

Enheduanna was the daughter of King Sargon of Akkad, the founder of one of the first empires in human history. He appointed Enheduanna as the high priestess of Sumeria. Her signature appears on a collection of hymns written for forty-two temples throughout the southern half of Mesopotamia. As such, she earned the honour of being the world's first author.

Just as predictable rhymes are cloyingly unpalatable, an overweening use of words decanted from thesaurus goblets in deliberately obscure sentences of free verse, gets irksome.

Since Enheduanna of Mesopotamia

(Poetry in the dock? Verse-Tradition versus Free-Verse)

In the beginning, was the word, and the word was with poetry
and the poetry was verse. Verse-Traditions' mnemonics
in rhyme and prosody help eternalise lines poetic.

Free-verse shatters shackles of the mind
to capture and imbibe, any fleeting thoughts,
mining the nuance, the sense, and the essence.

There are worse traditions than the Verse-Tradition
you resent, our learned Free-Verse friends
sometimes lapse into rhyme, for effect,

Attempting to explain.....what you're wondering.. they meant?

The oldest Verse-Traditions now classed as ex-tradition,
Extradite?... to which poetic jurisdiction? Replies
the prosecutor sternly...   where they commit cloying rhymes!

Free-Verse now approaches the witness stand,
unfettered, untrammelled, by beats, tweets or rhymes,
and plays to the gallery..... until the gavel.

Objection m'lord, free-verse knows no bounds,
messages relayed in lines, appearing well-hidden
reader and reason confounded in the maze

In conclusion m' lord.. there've been reams of dreams,
revolutions, national anthems, coronations... inspired by
verse-free and verse-tradition. On papyrus and parchment,

and paper and plasma.. since Enheduanna.. of Mesopotamia.
Verse-Traditions and Free-Verse..... will always coexist
may neither....... ever be compelled ...to cease and desist!

The Poet And Our Planet

the words of the poet do not stop at the lips,
they steer the soul. Poetry has forever been
at the heart of culture, each potent word
precisely aimed:- dominates, destroys or
dispels... a point, a subtext or a theme.

poetry bares the dirt, the deceit....the avarice
and the angst, just as it bursts asunder
fragrant, febrile, feelings ... of love, and lust?
vile, vindictive tyrants spitting vitriol
exposed in rhythm and rhyme and pace... and time.

earth's overpopulation starves in consternation
it's not the number of people but
the number of consumers, and the scale
and nature of consumption. The need to feed
must transcend..... the need for speed and greed.

twitter, youtube, facebook, arsefilm?
unwitting digital-arms-dealers
weaponising discourse in every form,
puppets sucked into... this 'performance culture'
blinded by fake news, views, likes and.... bland followers.

fucked-up minds and mindless heads
of state, purveyors of the bottom-line,
don't give a shit for a scorched earth
for those we leave behind, it's time the rest of us
try and assuage, every disastrous planet change.

PART TWO

A BRITISH POEM TRILOGY

The British East India Company (BEIC)
Birth of The British Raj
Demise of The British Raj

The only exceptions to the period under consideration in this collection are the three poems in this section "A British Poem Trilogy" —The British East India Company; Birth of The British Raj; Demise of The British Raj.

The British East India Company had its roots in India about two and a half centuries earlier. However, the impact of the events relating to these entities besides dominating global trade, permeated all aspects of our lives in the last twelve decades and hence justify inclusion.

The influence of the BEIC from 1601 to 1858 grew to such an extent that the company became the de facto governing authority throughout the territories of India.

The extremely fierce competition among European colonials to monopolise the lucrative trading profits from the East Indies, and particularly from India, was so intense that there were almost as many "East India Companies" set up, as there were European nations (Dutch, French, Swedish, Portuguese, Danish, Austrian, Genoese).

A realistic view of what the company hoped to achieve in India was perhaps even-handedly described in 1835 by Thomas Macaulay, a historian and a member of the ruling council of the BEIC. He said they expect to nurture "a class of persons, Indian in blood and colour, but English in taste, in opinions, in morals and in intellect" and he qualified that objective with a sentence that is often left out "it is impossible for us, with our limited means, to attempt to educate the body of the people"

The Company had spectacular success in terms of trade and had to focus on securing its interests. The three poems convey the sense of the lengths to which it went to win the competition and eventually paved the way for India to be the jewel in the crown of the British Empire.

The British East India Company (BEIC)

Although, officially, the British Government ruled India for just over eighty-nine years,
from 1858 to 1947, the British East India Company virtually owned, ruled and ran
India since 1601. That was the year when English merchants were authorised by
Queen Elizabeth 1 to trade in the East Indies. James Lancaster commanded the first
fleet of four ships that year, on an exploratory voyage. He returned in 1603 with a
cargo of 500 tons of peppercorn and was duly rewarded with a knighthood. For

decades their shareholders were raking it in hand-over-fist, the profits kept piling
but the Dutch East India Company's pepper cornered the spice trade and
pirates and wars began reducing their margins and shrinking their piles.
So the BEIC began cotton-picking in India, and then silk. Industrialisation built
textile mills in Britain, making skilled Indian weavers redundant, as mass-produced
clothing now available to all with Britain the world leader as the top textile trader.

By the mid-1700s, BEIC's interests were rapidly expanding, to protect all their assets,
they acquired their own armies. Under Robert Clive, attacking and annexing territories
of princes and nawabs as he deviously stripped them of their wealth by stealth.
Meanwhile, Europeans introduced to tea from China were asking for more and the
BEIC couldn't get enough as they were on a gold standard and China would only
Trade for silver. Answer... Grow opium in India and traffic it to China.

The British East India Company was... milking the tea in China
becoming the first international narcotics cartel to be ruthlessly involved
in the contraband opium war, readying to pay... for all the tea in China.

*"...there is a class of evil foreigner that makes opium and brings it for sale, tempting
fools to destroy themselves, merely in order to reap a profit."*

– Commissioner Lin Zexu, 1839

Birth of The British Raj

Maharajahs and princes no match for
operandi of conquest...subjugation..
swelled the coffers of the company,
financiers, keeping fashionistas in

his military might, Clive's modus
and forced-surrender to plunder,
fattening the City of London
sequins and silk with his warring

ventures in India. Winning the battle of
install..himself.. the Governor of Bengal.
tax and customs revenue and run police
relentlessly sown, providing the impetus

Plassey in 1757, then rushed to
So securing the right to collect
services and civil offices, seeds were
for an empire full blown.

Exit Robert Clive, a case of suicide...
property and valuables using loopholes
legal teams. The treasure ships escorted
Navy Czar, preventing the enrichment of

the Company continued usurping
in the law embedded by their own
back to blighty by Jack Tar, the Royal
pirates and rival Naval powers

The rapid expansion of the Company's
and rulers who resented the pace and
Banding together with Indian troops
started gathering momentum for

interests antagonised Indian princes
the imminent threat to their existence.
from the Company's army, soon
the Indian Rebellion of 1857.

The Atrocities from both sides made
The Crown very soon realise that
The Company was incapable of governing
The Sub-Continent.. and abolished it in 1858...
The Birth of The British Raj!

An extract from The Times "obituary" of the British East India Company, 2nd January 1874.

"It accomplished a work such as in the whole history of the human race no other Company ever attempted and as such, is ever likely to attempt in the years to come."

Demise of The British Raj

The victor writes the history, ergo – rarely
views have championed either
or Hitler's destruction of European
relinquished their colonies, and India

It is a fact that Gandhi's resistance got
support, and Hitler's Luftwaffe* had
Hungary, Denmark, Norway, Austria,
and were getting ready to breathe

on Normandy beaches. Churchill needed
and rescue the situation. Roosevelt refused
Britain would grant India independence
On receiving Churchill's assurance he

FDR's principled decision was based on
..the peace to follow cannot include any
peace demands and will get equality
conceded Franklin was right, and bowed

Britain's economy after the war was brought
kept nipping at its heels. Britain, cap in hand,
Marshall Plan**, India now an unaffordable
ornament – just ointment. Parliament was

objective. For decades entrenched
Gandhi's non-violent methods
economies, as the reason colonials
to have gained its independence.

worldwide exposure and some lukewarm
beaten the shit out of Czechoslovakia,
Belgium, the Netherlands and France
down the necks of the allied forces

President Franklin D Roosevelt to step in
any help unless Churchill agreed that
and to its other colonies worldwide.
gave the greenlight to the US Air Force.

his dislike of a *"backward colonial policy*
continued despotism. The structure of
of peoples". Churchill was peeved, but
to the wisdom of a perceptive mind.

to its knees. The Indian National Congress
received the largest largesse from the
jewel – just a fly, and the crown no
forced to shoo away the fly.

On 15th, August 1947
India got its independence....
the demise of the British Raj!

Luftwaffe*　　　　– German Air Force
Marshall Plan**　– The Western European Recovery Initiative (US Aid) advocated by
　　　　　　　　　George C Marshall, US Secretary of Defence, to help these countries'
　　　　　　　　　economies to recover after World War ll

The British media was annoyed that Roosevelt had held out until he got assurance from Churchill, that he would not pursue the colonial ambitions of Britain after the war. Hitler was within hours of winning at Normandy when he was stopped by the intervention of the US Airforce.

However, the true feelings between the two leaders can be understood from their comments below:

Franklin and Winston

What they said:

> *"I think I speak as America's President when I say that America won't help England in this war simply so that she will be able to continue to ride roughshod over colonial peoples.*
>
> *I can't believe that we can fight a war against fascist slavery and at the same time not work to free people all over the world from a backward colonial policy ... the peace cannot include any continued despotism.*
>
> *The structure of peace demands and will get equality of peoples."*
>
> – President Franklin Delano Roosevelt

When Franklin D Roosevelt suddenly died (12 April 1945), the following paragraph from Winston Churchill's eulogy captures the depth of respect and admiration that he had gradually developed for FDR:

> *"For us. it remains only to say that in Franklin D. Roosevelt there died the greatest American friend we have ever known and the greatest champion of freedom who has ever brought help and comfort from the new world to the old."*
>
> – Prime Minister Winston Leonard Spencer-Churchill

PART THREE
CLIMATE CHANGE SONNETS

Some notes about Shakespearean Sonnets:

In all there are records of 154 Shakespeare sonnets.

In this collection, all of the sonnets follow the favoured structure of the 'king of bards' himself.

The total number of lines in the sonnet are fourteen. They are arranged in three sets of four lines and a final one of two lines.

Each set of four lines is a quatrain and the final set is the couplet.

The meter or rhythm of these sonnets is the iambic pentameter. An iamb is a foot of two syllables – a soft followed by a hard syllable. Every line has five (penta) feet with a total of exactly ten syllables to a line.

An example of an iamb or a foot:

Sonnet 12

When I / do COUNT / the CLOCK / that TELLS / the TIME
Each foot has two syllables the soft syllable followed by the hard (shown in CAPITALS)

A foot needn't be made of a complete word, or words.

The following two examples from Shakespear's sonnets show how a single word can be part of two different feet:

Sonnet 18

Shall I / com PARE/ thee TO / a SUM / mer's DAY?
Thou ART / more LOVE / ly AND / more TEM / per ATE

Summer's – a SUM / mer's DAY – the two feet are: a SUM / mer's DAY;

Lovely – more LOVE / ly AND – the two feet are: more LOVE / ly AND;

Sonnet 29

When IN / dis GRACE / with FOR / tune AND / men's EYES
I ALL / a LONE / be WEEP / my OUT / cast STATE

Fortune – with FOR / tune AND – the two feet are: with FOR / tune AND

Outcast – my OUT / cast STATE – the two feet are: my OUT / cast STATE

And finally, Shakespearean sonnets have a rhyming sequence that is structured as follows:

1st Quatrain :   abab
2nd Quatrain :   cdcd
3rd Quatrain :   efef

Couplet :   gg

Individual Messages.... in a sonnet:

In order to convey the visceral and emotional urgency that comes across when these passionate individuals convey their messages, I have sculpted, verbatim, some of the expressions/phrases uttered by them into their respective sonnets.

David Attenborough

Dodos, and deniers of climate change science and other sciences for that matter, have never fully appreciated the honesty of this man. A renowned naturalist, devoted to the wellbeing of both humans and every aspect of nature with non-negotiable integrity.

Sir David Frederick Attenborough, who is now in the 95th year of his existence on this planet that he dearly loves, has very little to gain whether or not humanity and all other creatures on earth today, and those to appear in the future, still enjoy a habitable earth. Yet, his desire to enlighten us about the gravity of our situation is so altruistic that he travels even today, to remote and challenging environments to present the facts, in real time, about the irreversible damage we are causing to our planet.

The David Attenborough Message... in a sonnet

Climate change – it's taking place here and now
First time in history we can witness
Impacts of climate change where, when and how
Obstinate leaders created this mess

We see climate changes in real-time
Huge storms, floods, heatwaves, and sea-levels rise
Ignorant cynics are truly the prime
Reason the planet is nearing demise

Let's be clear, it's happening in your world
It's happening in my world, it will get
A lot worse as more disasters unfurl
Extinction now a vow – not just a threat

   Science has evidence clear and distinct
   We must act quick or risk being extinct

Brian Cox

If ever there was recognition endorsed by a hallowed individual to a worthy successor then this statement by Sir David Attenborough about Professor Brian Cox is a prime example: "If I had a torch I would hand it to Brian Cox"

Brian Cox, the former Pop Star turned Particle Physics Professor, has been wowing international audiences with his spellbinding series of natural history documentaries.

Essentially, Brian's expertise in the sciences, when explained by him in clear, concise and engaging TV episodes, helps the layperson understand, appreciate and respect the wonders of our world.

The Brian Cox Message... in a sonnet

Unlike in the past, we can now observe
Climate disasters and devastation
Throughout the planet and without reserve
We have let our planet face extinction

The oceans are the best thermometer
We have for the planet, we plainly see
Global warming making our earth hotter
There is no place to hide on land or sea

Don't undermine the science just because
You don't like the economics and hence
You underplay effects and not the cause
Your stupid attitude is just nonsense

   The evidence from science is quite clear
   Take action now before we disappear

Greta Thunberg

Just two years ago, Greta Thunberg made history when at the age of 15 she started her one-girl protest outside the Swedish parliament buildings. This solitary stand of a frail teenage girl set her on the path to confront the most powerful people on earth. Her message to them was clear and delivered with passion "Take urgent action now to slow down and stop the irreversible damage that we are causing to our planet."

The reason most individuals give for not doing anything to change their way of life is that it will not make a difference if the other 7 billion people on earth do nothing about it. Alas, there is a moral imperative for every one of us to do something about it right now. Remember just one example, it is the climate-strike students who passed on their words and actions in their communities and are now seen as the biggest threat to the large and powerful oil conglomerates. Examples set by the few do get followed by the many.

A potent metaphor I have heard used is that if I took a bulldozer and razed the crops of a subsistence farmer in a third world country, you would immediately say that I was wrong and that I should stop it **right now**. That, however, is exactly what I am doing when I refuse to lower my emissions in a prosperous country like the UK. Just because the gases are invisible and there is a time delay, doesn't permit me to 'exercise' my right to freedom of action because... **it does not extend to harming others**.

That is the nub of Greta's message.

The Greta Thunberg Message... in a sonnet

My name is Greta Thunberg, I'm sixteen
Years old and come from Sweden. I speak for
The future generations who are keen
To shock you 'fore this planet is no more

But I don't want your hope, I don't want you
To be hopeful. I want you to panic,
Feel the fear I feel everyday anew
It's a crisis you climate-change cynic

I was lucky to be born in a place
And time, when everyone told us to dream
Big, and fulfill our ambitions apace
An attitude so crass, it makes us scream

   For thirty years you had time to be spurred
   And yet our voices are not being heard

Plain Dead

Plastic may break down in time because of wind, waves, and the sun but it is never destroyed.

It keeps getting ripped to shreds or shattered into tiny particles which eventually end up as microplastics. The pollution it causes results in a worldwide environmental crisis.

These are some staggering figures from reliable, responsible and respected sources about the environmental devastation that our use of plastic is causing to whales, dolphins, porpoises, and other creatures living in our oceans.

Between 4 and 13 million metric tonnes of plastic appear every year floating on the surface of oceans, sunk to the seabed or washed up ashore on beaches. Very realistic estimates point to the fact that we have, in the last 60 years produced in excess of 8.3 billion tonnes of plastic.

Plain dead!

a thoughtless act discards
the empty pack
of crisps o'er board
think no more of it you litter lout

you ought to see the plight... the sorry sight
of the pilot whale cajoling
her lifeless cub to draw a breath
a twitch.. a quiver.. is enough

to raise her forlorn hopes but   it's dead!
not playing dead..... plain dead!

the crisp packet, coffee cup and
shopping bag enmeshed
within the ocean's garbage patch
swirling around the five ocean gyres

in time break down and slivers of
plastic ingested by the whale
poisoned the milk she fed the cub
resulting in stillbirth

mama whale for several days
Propped her cub
So it wouldn't sink
To the plastic dump that...   took its life

In denial......   that her treasured cub
Is dead!

Not playing dead....plain dead!

Sixty Percent Extinct

Human activity is directly responsible for the extinction of our fellow creatures on this planet. In the last fifty years from 1970 to 2020, humans have decimated more than sixty percent of them, while our human population has grown from 3 billion to 7 billion – a record breaking increase in the history of our species.

Expressed another way – it's not because more babies are being born on the planet but because fewer humans are leaving the planet i.e. not dying – we are living longer. This appears to be a double-edged sword – we have overcome many of the diseases that were killing our ancestors but our longevity necessitates the use of ever increasing land to grow food.

The area of the Earth needed for the resources an individual requires and to remove their waste products is called their 'ecological footprint' which is a measure of their impact on the environment, and is well publicised. At present, each human's ecological footprint is 2.3 hectares of land which is more than the size of three football pitches. The World Commission on Environment and Development estimates that the available productive land for an individual is only 1.7 hectares. Which confirms that considerable numbers of human beings' lifestyles are not sustainable.

The Sixty Percent (Sonnet)

Sixty percent of mammals, birds, insects,
Reptiles and fish made extinct by mankind
In just fifty years... compare the effects
If sixty percent of humans declined

It would effectively mean emptying
Africa, Europe, Oceania
In addition you would be excluding
The whole of North and South America

Consuming the Earth's future resources
For short term lifestyle gains is a gamble
This concern should engage our discourses
Without cynics who blather and ramble

  A third of land acutely degraded
  It's crucial that it's not left unaided

PART FOUR
CULTURAL IMPACT

Cultural customs and practices through the centuries have been passed down to successive generations forming the thread that knits the fabric of society. From the smallest family units to communities, villages, towns, cities and nations there is social bonding that embraces togetherness, which in turn becomes the identity of a particular unit.

A flipside of this, unfortunately, is 'ethnocentrism' when one believes that one's own culture is superior to that of another using your own cultural ideals as a yardstick.

A more balanced judgement for harmony is 'cultural relativism' where one tries to understand the context in which a particular custom has been absorbed and is practised.

Cultural practices can also have detrimental effects on members within a society. The victims are usually those who do not or cannot comply with the prevailing customs, views and even baseless beliefs enshrined in law and rigidly followed by the majority .

I have curated three poems that illustrate how much, and how little, has changed in the last twelve decades, in terms of altering the lives of people for the better despite the remarkable advances in our knowledge in various fields of learning.

Of the three poems in this section, the first poem "Yours in distress" is a Shakespearean sonnet about Alan Turing: mathematician; philosopher; acknowledged father of computer science. He was reviled by the British Legal System for his homosexuality in the 1940s and '50s.

The second poem "The Dalit's Wife" is about the abominable caste system that dehumanises millions of the lowest caste (the untouchables) Indians who are destined for generations to face blatant segregation and menial jobs like cleaning dry latrines.

The final poem in the section is about "Margaret Sanger". This remarkable woman who had lost seven of her siblings and her mother to an early grave, because a reliable source of contraception was unavailable to women.

Alan Turing
Yours in distress

(Alan Turing's last letter to his fellow mathematician, Norman Routledge,
before pleading guilty)

"I'm afraid that the following syllogism may be used by some in the future.

Turing believes machines think
Turing lies with men
Therefore machines do not think

Yours in distress,
Alan"

Alan Turing
Yours In Distress (Sonnet)

Ancient laws destroying women and men
Imprisoned body, broke spirit and will
To live. An honest, beautiful mind then
Chose castration rather than rot in jail.

Ignorance and superstition gone mad
Bedevilled innocent Turing throughout
The broken code-breaker finally had
To learn what the witch hunt was all about.

The chemical treatment addled his brain,
Rejecting life in a world without love.
His struggles with nature now under strain
With no help on this earth or from above.

  This true patriot having to decide
  Bid farewell by committing suicide

The Dalit's Wife

(Dalit = untouchables)

The fact that the most inhuman, undignified, and barbaric caste system exists on earth today, is a travesty of social justice and human decency.

India, the largest of the South Asian countries, with staggering inaction throughout the millennium, has tacitly helped continue the social, political and cultural obscenity of casteism. Periodic tinkering with the statutes and laws have produced no results at all.

Even today, human beings are involved in physically transporting human excreta alongside the supersonic flights, 5G Wifi, nuclear power and space travel – that's just ludicrous.

The Dalit's Wife

the foetor didn't just waft, it belched.... into the space
consuming the entrails of the hut
the zig-zag snaking chawls and cul-de-sacs
like apocrine glands secreting into the smelly armpit
of this dalit universe.

the ramshackle of an euphemized home
in the dalit neighbourhood....
desensitising olfactory nerve endings
of this western social worker ?
it doesn't... I retch

millions of dalits inhabit this earth
barbaric 15th c BC caste system
brutally strangling 21st c AD humans – the victims – dalits:
the scum of society – porters of night soil...
carrying away human shit

on their heads, in palm-leaf baskets, mostly women,
a broom of straw, a plate of tin,
the basket filled, she walks the miles, leaking
drips of shit trickle down her face, she throws up....
with saree's end.... she mops her lips.. and the drips

such indignity exists today, forced
upon the lowliest – born.. to.. be.. ground.. down..
the.. dry.. latrine – intellectual sophistry?
what's in a name? Dalits or Achhoot, the untouchables
renamed Harijan – God's children –

God give her strength!... to endure this filthy
punishment. Her husband's corpse lay where he fell
labouring for the village Patil. A dalit's corpse
less dignified than a carcass in an abattoir.
This dalit corpse is left to rot... with flesh ripped off
........by straying dogs.

Margaret Sanger

The contraceptive pill was approved in 1960 in the US for married women but took a further 10 years until 1970 when it was made available for unmarried women. That's when the economic revolution of the last century really started. In the US it was the contraceptive of choice for 18 and 19-year-old women. Women were choosing careers in every field of endeavour as they had complete control over their reproductive calendars and could choose when to have their babies.

While we are in this section that deals with culture, it is worth noting as an example, how cultural attitudes can impact the economic and other progress parameters of a nation. Japan, a technology-savvy nation which was a more male-dominated society in the 1960s than the US, did not approve the pill for unmarried women until 1999, a good 39 years after it was first approved in the US. Needless to say, Japan's economy was greatly hampered because their culture was holding back the growth of their economy, by withholding the same opportunities for women that the use of the pill was affording women in other developed countries.

Margaret Sanger and that Magic Pill

(aka "The Woman Rebel")

From the other side of the coffin she stared into her father's eyes
His wife, her mother – its inhabitant "You caused this – Mother is dead from
Having too many children."... his vacant stare expressed his abject sufferance
In twenty-two years she had eighteen pregnancies, seven stillbirths and eleven childbirths

Margaret was the sixth, she was now nineteen her mother, dead at fifty.. in that coffin.
Do numbers count? Yes, countless babies do... the lack of space, the overcrowding, the
Hungry nights and hungrier days she'd visit girls, women, destitutes and prostitutes
To educate them, all the while just dreaming.... of that "magic pill"

A qualified nurse, she'd treated women after back-alley abortions and self-terminated
pregnancies. In 1912 wrote in her newspaper column "What Every Girl Should Know"
Tirelessly pursuing her one passionate aim "No woman can call herself free until
she can choose consciously... whether she will or will not be a mother."

Gregory Pincus, a human reproduction expert, was approached by Sanger with funds
from Katharine McCormick the heiress of the International Harvester, this
teamwork helped develop the first oral contraceptive, Enovid,
Approved by the Food and Drug Administration on June 23, 1960.

In women's emancipatory terms this date is most significant, for the first time in
human history, women could choose not to have babies they did not want, while
continuing to have the sex they did want. Sanger's work had one clear message:

"Every child should be a wanted child"

PART FIVE

POLITICS, SOCIETY, CULTURE,
AND
NOTABLE INDIVIDUALS

World War One (WW I)
(28 July, 1914 – 11 November, 1918)

Background/Context

Bosnia and Herzegovina, the dual provinces in the volatile Balkan region of Europe and part of the Ottoman Empire, were annexed by the dual monarchy of the Austro-Hungarian Empire on 6th October, 1908. A Bosnian Serb revolutionary committed to ending the Austro-Hungarian rule shot and killed the heir presumptive to the throne, Archduke Franz Ferdinand and his wife Duchess Sophia Hohenberg as they were driving through the capital city of Sarajevo to inspect the forces on the 28th of June, 1914.

This solitary act was the spark that set off a chain reaction within Europe, and beyond, with countries aligning themselves with one of the two main camps: the Central (Axis) Powers/Forces and the Allied Powers/Forces. Other countries in the region were minor players whose loyalty to either of the camps was not as strong. World War 1 was officially declared a month later on the 28th of July, 1914.

Central Powers: Austria-Hungary, Germany, the Ottoman Empire and Bulgaria

Allied Powers: Britain, France, Russia, Belgium and the United States

The World War One (WW1) Sonnet

Gavrilo Princip the Serb assassin
Craved to end Austro-Hungarian rule
An act the world could never imagine
Discussing for years at work, play and school

The killing of Franz Ferdinand and wife
On the streets of Sarajevo triggered
World War 1, the carnage and loss of life
Leaving Europe defiled and disfigured

And seventeen million people were dead
The rape of Belgium an atrocity
by the Germans, just mayhem and bloodshed
Of which, Allied Powers too were guilty

    This war was referred to as 'The Great War'
    And, wrongfully, "a war to end all wars"

Hiroshima and Nagasaki
(when the living.....envied their dead)

I am writing this backstory and poem in the week 6th to 13th, August, 2020 — the 75th anniversary of the bombing of the Japanese cities of Hiroshima and Nagasaki in 1945 on 6th, August and 9th, August respectively. I have gone into some detail here because the atrocities committed and versions of events recorded are often given partisan slants, for obvious reasons, by the countries involved.

The poem distilled from books, media coverage of this anniversary and my research, describes the collective physical and mental horror that was experienced by the victims of the only two nuclear bombs that have been detonated during warfare. The poetosuggestive message extruded is one of absolute abhorrence to even the faintest idea of using a nuclear bomb... ever again. Big ask? I know.

In the mid-nineteenth century, following the discoveries of far-off lands by european navigators/explorers, colonial expansion was rampant as Western powers began breaking up regions of China and other countries of Asia to establish their dominance.

Japan decided it was time to join the fray and soon was able to compete for dominance of the Asian mainland. They succeeded in winning the battles for dominating Korea against China in 1895 and against Russia in 1905.

An increasingly belligerent Japan, with ambitions of expanding its empire, invaded Manchuria in 1931 and China in 1937 and continued these onslaughts by invading and moving into French Indochina in 1940. Spurred on by these successes, Japan joined the Axis Tripartite Pact with Italy and Germany in 1941.

As the world stood aghast at these developments, President Roosevelt decided to act by imposing a trade embargo on scrap steel and oil going to Japan from America for the use of the Japanese military. The people in America, however, were not willing to go to war in distant Asia to stop Japan's militaristic ventures.

The US policy was unchanged after the "Rape of Nanking" in 1937, when tens of thousands of Chinese women were raped by the Japanese forces, and even after the Japanese military murdered up to 200,000 helpless Chinese military prisoners and civilians – scores of them, gratuitously, in one "killing contest" (two army officers competed to see how quickly they could kill 100 Chinese people with one sword each, not necessarily in combat).

Japan figured if they could win the Dutch and British colonies then they could get all the oil, rubber and raw materials that they badly needed and that only the Pacific forces of the Americans could stop them.

Admiral Yamamoto of the Japanese navy displayed exceptional tactical acuity when he stealthily managed to surprise the US Naval fleet based at Pearl Harbour, by sailing his own aircraft carriers within range, and then mounting an all-out preemptive attack on December 7, 1941. The US fleet's battleships and carriers were virtually decimated. This attack made the US population rise up as one and fully supported President Roosevelt's decision to join WWII, a few years later.

That was the date Roosevelt referred to on the following day – saying that it will be remembered as "a day of infamy". In the ensuing three years Japan was still attempting to make gains in the Pacific theatre of war and this time the American population were firmly behind Roosevelt's decision to join the allied forces in WWII to help Britain.

Roosevelt's sudden death on 12th April, 1945 brought Harry Truman into the White House and despite his demands for an unconditional surrender, as Japan's military stood no chance against the US atom bomb, Japan refused.

Truman said he made the decision to drop Little Boy (uranium gun-type atomic bomb) on Hiroshima to force an unconditional surrender immediately and so stop the war and destruction of other Japanese cities – but the Japan War Council refused to surrender. So after another thirty-six-hour wait the second atomic bomb Fat Man (an implosion-type nuclear weapon with a solid plutonium core) was dropped on Nagasaki – this forced Emperor Hirohito to overrule resistance from some members of the War Council and the Emperor surrendered – unconditionally.

Even though Hitler had shot himself May 8, 1945, and the Germans surrendered, the unconditional surrender from Japan only came on August 15, 1945 – and the Second World War officially ended. This date is now celebrated globally as VJ Day or Victory over Japan Day.

Hiroshima and Nagasaki

Thrust between the nuclear blast and fallout shelters, the frantic
millions exhausted and forlorn, await their fate.
Their spirits crushed, the darkness dares to tease... the flashing laser
scimitars bouncing, cavorting, shapes in fatalistic guile.

Released energy of the nuclear blast, lethality much greater than
a chemical explosion, dissipated through pulses of energy
electrical and magnetic – the electromagnetic pulse (EM P) instantly
razing to the ground most structures and killing thousands...the lucky ones?

The hibakusha* left to endure gruesome mutilation
from the blast. Shrapnel-cracked heads – exposing brains; slashed bellies -
intestines; raw skin cleanly peeling off the flesh – glowing, weeping, seeping,
serum and plasma bubbling – victims of thermal radiation.....

wishing... they weren't alive...... nuclear radiation causing
immediate, short and long term diseases of internal organs,
prospects of lingering terminal illnesses for years,
pain and suffering in their nuked homes and cities

....it's when the living..... envied their dead!

*hibakusha = survivors

World War Two (WW2)

Background/Context

Key events that unfurled after the first world war "the war to end all wars" had, in fact, provided the animus between various countries and revived political aspirations of imperial supremacy. The meteoric rise of the Nazi Party in Germany with Hitler at the helm in 1933, pushing his aggressive foreign policy while in Italy fascism had been gaining a hold since the 1920s and the Japanese were flexing their muscles in China — these smouldering developments along with other smaller skirmishes contributed to the gathering storm of hostility between the nations.

World War Two (WW2)

**The most destructive war in Human History
(1st September 1939 – 2nd September 1945)**

At the Munich Agreement
Hitler's opening gambit
Insisting Czechoslovakia be split
And part-annexed...... a ploy to test the resolve
Of Chamberlain in a possible face-off
Of who blinks first? Britain sadly did

Chamberlain so badly wanted to avoid
Another war so soon after the first
He was over the moon as he waved
His paper for the crowds to see, "Peace for our time"
He shouted, gullibly trusting the words of Hitler
Pity he hadn't read – the Fuehrer's "Mein Kampf"

The foreign office said, Hitler couldn't be trusted
Chamberlain was bent on wanting to appease him
He finally gave in to all of Hitler's demands
Better Hitler than Stalin at the channel ports?
For Nazism was preferable to Communism
While Hitler kept plotting his German Empire

Chamberlain's speech after the 'no confidence' vote:
"Everything I have worked for,
everything that I have hoped for,
everything that I have believed in
during my public life, has crashed into ruins."
And with that he resigned making way for Winston

Churchill stepped up to the plate, by popular demand,
"Cometh the hour, cometh the man"
His decision to fight and not negotiate
Was endorsed by the house and the work began
Against Hitler's advances the allies stood firm
Finally winning the war at an extortionate price

Millions were dying, dead, injured and maimed
By air raids, rockets, blitzkrieg invasions,
commando raids. Cities and towns set ablaze
and razed to the ground, scorched fields
and death camps reminding humanity the depths
to which humans had sunk... in the 20th century.

Helmuth Hubener

(The boy who 'didn't give a fuck for Hitler')

When the boy scouts of Germany were disbanded to be absorbed into
The Hitler Youth, who along with Nazi sympathisers took part in Kristallnacht,
Crystal Night or The Night Of Broken Glass, the pogrom against the German jews –
Helmuth Hubener was disgusted. At thirteen, had the balls to say 'fuck the Fuehrer'
........And left The Hitler Youth

Hitler's bombastic radio broadcasts lying, that Germany was going to win the war
while the BBC (German) broadcasts relayed the facts disputing Hitler's lies,
Helmuth Hubener was listening to this forbidden channel, on his older-
brother's radio huddled in a closet in the hallway.

He heard the truth that the allied forces were on the brink of a resounding victory,
determined to let the people know the truth, with two best friends the trio wrote, printed,
and distributed, pamphlets exhorting Germans to rise up and resist the Fuehrer,
Helmuth's sense of fairness, moral rectitude, justice and human dignity would shame

The army generals who, so slavishly obeyed unconscionable orders to
commit genocide when millions of jews were killed for just being born into
a jewish family – the abominable crimes driven by – a warped belief in the Aryan
Master Race? with a Master Plan? Go Masturbate!

Down with Hitler, Hitler the Murderer, *The Voice of Conscience, Who is lying?*
these pamphlets spread the word but soon The Gestapo had Helmuth behind bars
then tried by the *Volksgerichtshof the verdict....... "Death by beheading"

Hubener bravely placed his head on the chopping block........
The Guillotine at Seventeen!

(Born: 8th January, 1925 – Beheaded: 27th October, 1942)

*Volksgerichtshof = The infamous "People's Court", mainly courts run by the Nazi party.

Hannah Arendt

When Hannah died in 1975, she was still the only woman promoted as full professor at Princeton. She was an internationally acclaimed woman political theorist in an environment that, at the time, generally discriminated against her gender. When asked how she felt about being a woman professor, she replied "I am not at all disturbed about being a woman professor because I am quite used to being a woman."

Hannah Arendt, today, is deservedly recognised as one of the exceptional thinkers of the last century. In fact, her perceptive foresight about "dark times" which besides addressing the distressing consequences of twentieth-century totalitarianism, brings us face-to-face with our current global situations in the twenty-first century. Hannah asserted that "If it is the function of the public realm to throw light on the affairs of men by providing a space of appearances in which they can show in deed and word, for better or worse, who they are and what they can do, then darkness has come when this light is extinguished by 'credibility gaps' and 'invisible government,' by speech that does not disclose what is, but sweeps it under the carpet, by exhortations, moral and otherwise, that under the pretext of upholding old truths, degrade all truth in meaningless triviality."

"Fake news" travelling at internet speed and 'fact check' languishing at human speed seem to have proved her fears well founded as we are witnessing the consequences in every digital form of discourse today, the main difference being, today it is no longer a meaningless triviality but a nuclear time-bomb that could be set off by unthinking, crass and psychopathic leadership that is scattered throughout the continents.

Shortly after Hannah arrived in New York, she cheekily wrote in an article that the 20th century had created a type of human being – "*the kind that are put into concentration camps by their foes and internment camps by their friends*".

The Hannah Arendt Sonnet

Arendt, now with 20/20 hindsight
Clearly stands out as a leading thinker
In the twentieth century spotlight
Recognition that certainly suits her

Her prescient notion about "dark times"
Scorning totalitarianism
Very relevant to these days – it chimes
With our conflicts and turmoil and schisms

A global upheaval of governments
Dismantling time honoured institutions
With bluff, bluster, and tweets of false statements
Hannah's "dark times" are here – no delusions

    The motto of some world leaders today
    Distort facts, whatever you do or say.

Gorbachev's Gamble

The botched attempt by the US in 1960, to overthrow Fidel Castro's communist regime by training cuban exiles from the US, prompted the Russian President, Nikita Krushchev, to help Castro survive the coup and retain his rule. Krushchev also went further and secretly offered Fidel Castro support to thwart any further attempts by the US to interfere with the government of Cuba.

The game of 'chicken' inherited by the US President, John Fitzgerald Kennedy (from Dwight D Eisenhower) against the 'russian roulette' dare from Nikita Krushchev, mercifully ended without the dreaded outcome of a nuclear confrontation.

Although the theatre of war was the uncannily named "Bay of Pigs" on the southwestern coast of Cuba, in October 1962, every move and countermove was personally authorised by these two individuals located, respectively, in the White House and the Kremlin, with negligible input from advisers.

Following this near nuclear-disaster, future leaders of both these nuclear powers were forced to consider very carefully the possibility of an accidental global catastrophe as a result of misunderstanding or the deliberate actions of the first-strike-advantage-seeking aggressor.

Even though US President, Lyndon Baines Johnson initiated arms control talks with the Soviet leader Alexei N Kosygin in June 1967, and three successive US Presidents, Richard Nixon, Gerald R. Ford and Jimmy Carter, consecutively signed strategic-arms limitation agreements (SALT talks) with the perennial Soviet President, Leonid I Brezhnev, it was President, Mikhail Sergeyvich Gorbachev, of the Soviet Republic who had the foresight and the courage to take the initiative and react warmly to the overtures of US President, Ronald Reagan. Together they took down 'The Iron curtain'.

Gorbachev's Gamble

(Mikhail Sergeyvich Gorbachev)

The son of a peasant, a distant, far cry, from humble beginnings in Stavropol Krai*
rose to the pinnacle of the behemoth, sluggish, gigantean, secretive system.
A breath of fresh air as he set about tearing down rigid structures. Doing business
with Kohl, the Iron Lady and Reagan the Berlin Wall tumbled down, and then he got rid

of the Iron Curtain. Glasnost's openness emboldened him to take on the Augean task
of reforming the broken and battered economy, he was the architect and enabler
of Perestroika's restructuring. The empty supermarket shelves a disgrace, in the eyes
of the world, yet apparatchiks* kicked, and screamed, every step of the way.

He saw how his people in the USSR were impoverished and miserable, compared
to the west, the State was controlling every aspect of life, he didn't think it was right
and resisted brazen opposition, by injecting the idea that this was the start
of a long term solution, to address the ills of communist principles.

The Chernobyl explosion was the point at which, Gorbachev came to the conclusion
that nuclear warfare would be disastrous for the world, regardless of who used
the first strike advantage. He saw vast areas of Belarus, Ukraine and Russia
that were affected – spreading into Europe and remote Canada. Gorbachev decided

To meet Ronald Reagan!

Stavropol Krai* = a part of Southern Russia located in the North Caucasus region and is governed by the North Caucasian Federal District.

Apparatchiks* = officials/bureaucrats within the communist party

Nelson Mandela

(18 July 1918 – 5 December 2013)

Nelson Mandela was born and brought up in a South Africa, where all his ancestors were frustratingly aware that many whites considered the blacks as a separate breed: subhuman; inferior; and undeserving of any human consideration. Yes, it was that stark.

The whites in power did not think of blacks as people with the same hopes, desires and aspirations as those of the whites. The entire legal framework was skewed in a way that afforded no means, whatsoever, for blacks to ever achieve, even a semblance of equality, in any aspect of normal citizenry. Every avenue of opportunity towards advancement was shut to them. Residential areas, parks and public transport, places of recreation, restaurants and hotels were "legally" barred or segregated.

Most blacks and some enlightened whites with integrity, knew this was wrong. The African National Congress (ANC) had avowed non-violent legal methods for opposing the tyrannical, oppressive and exploitative laws such as: separating husband and wife as they were not allowed to live in white neighbourhood areas, where only men would live to work on black-designated outskirts of white areas. The dreaded pass laws which were readily abused with illegal imprisonments and death sentences with no recourse, whatsoever, to fairness and justice.

As every attempt to legally resist the abominable laws that promoted white supremacy were thwarted by white supremacists, Mandela, and the ANC began adopting some violence as a last resort because accepting white supremacy implied black inferiority. That to Nelson Mandela, who had resisted both the idea of white domination and the idea of black domination, was non-negotiable.

He was fortunate in finding an honest and upright white individual in F W De Klerk, who was courageous enough to reject the abominable demands of his white supremacist party that wanted to continue apartheid in South Africa, for as long as they could maintain their supremacy. De Klerk held a free and fair election in 1990 and the ANC won the election,

Mandela's words in his speech on 20th April, 1964, captures the essence of the man:

> *"I have cherished the ideal of a democratic and free society in which all persons live together in harmony and with equal opportunities. It is an ideal which I hope to live for and to achieve. But if need be, it is an ideal for which I am prepared to die."*

> – Nelson Mandela

Nelson Mandela (Sonnet)

Although he was born to nobility
his skin pigmentation was wrong – not white
whites weren't ready to face reality
but facts on the ground were shining their light

when peaceful means failed and forced to take arms
Mandela insisted 'one man, one vote'
arrested and exiled on grazing farms
of Robben Island, he worked from remote

De Klerk held a free and fair election
to form a multiracial government
the overwhelming support for Nelson
finally got him declared President

　　De Klerk and Mandela.. joy in their eyes,
　　they had jointly won the Nobel Peace Prize!

9/11 – Twin Towers And Beyond

Rita Kempley of The Washington Post said "if we erase the towers from our art, we erase it from our memories".

This event changed the dynamics of global travel.

9/11

Terror at Twin Towers and surrounds

The worst terror attack ever on US soil,
orchestrated in morbid pilot-plots,
flying four passenger planes back-to-back
most victims had no chance... death was their lot.

The north and south towers of the World Trade Centre,
attacked by two exocets in quick surgical strikes
slicing them cleanly – decapitated towers?.... then
dust, burning aviation fuel and lethal missiles from

free-flying debris. The mix forming dark clouds of
billowing smoke – people dazed, fazed, falling out of
windows, some scrambling others resigned, a count of
around 200 dead bodies, were swept off

the ground. Emergency services personnel rushed
through the flames, assisting people trapped
transiting offices, stair wells and lifts. While concrete cracked,
tempered, twisted metal rods and sheets hampered

access to the injured needing help, these selfless
acts of duteous care causing greatest loss of life
among devoted personnel. These most audacious attacks
around surrounds as well, changed our way of life

with about three thousand dead.

Creepy Totalitarianism

The speed of change, rendering our world unfathomable has made us aware, for some time now, that we have been inured to beliefs that nothing is true and that everything is possible. We now find ourselves so polarised and in awe of our leaders that even when tangible evidence is provided, to prove the falsity of a ludicrous statement or an outrageous action by a leader, their staunch supporters will cynically look for any tenuous link to claim their leader just played a masterstroke of gamesmanship.

Hannah Arendt, in The Origins of Totalitarianism so pithily pointed out:

> "The ideal subject of totalitarian rule is not the convinced Nazi or the convinced Communist, but people for whom the distinction between fact and fiction (the reality of experience) and the distinction between true and false (the standards of thought) no longer exist".

Creepy Totalitarianism (Sonnet)

(aka "The blurring of fact and fiction")

This fickle, incomprehensible world
Allows the masses to reach the point where
Both truth and lie are equally unfurled
On cyber media to like and share

If next day there's irrefutable proof
Of their falsehood, they take a cynical
View and say they were aware of the spoof
Praising leaders for being tactical

While fake news travels at internet speed
Whizzing the lie around the globe and back
Human speed fact checks cannot take the lead
In killing the lie stone-dead in its track

    Their die-hard supporters always insist
    Difference in true and false doesn't exist

Emily Wilding Davison

Until the Representation of the People Act 1918, British women and men with no property, didn't have the right to vote. Even the act did not actually change much because now it allowed men without property over the age of 21, and only women over 30, to vote. It was not until ten years later that equality was achieved in 1928 when women over the age of 21 could also vote.

Emily Wilding Davison and the WSPU

the firebrand of the Women's Social and Political Union,
the suffragette Emily Wilding Davison, single-mindedly
pursued her belief in 'emancipation not empowerment'
the latter being passive, the former active she went for it
full-steam ahead – much to the tut-tut of some suffragettes

after Kensington High School, a bursary to Royal Holloway College,
next a gap year to earn money then enrolled at St Hugh's College at
Oxford, achieving first-class honours in English – yet deprived of
Graduation because Oxford degrees were closed to women.
This blatant unfairness just hardened her resolve to end the travesty

of patriarchal monopoly. Even Sylvia, the daughter of Emmeline
Pankhurst, described Davison as "one of the most daring and reckless
of the militants". Her disruptive actions.....chaining to rails, smashing
windows, setting ablaze postboxes, obstructing traffic and disrupting
men-only political meetings, result....a series of arrests, hunger strikes

and force-feedings. Armed with two suffragette flags of purple, white
and green she travelled to the Epsom Derby June 4, 1913... and
positioned herself at the final bend before the home straight. As the
Horses passed her she ducked under the barrier to approach King George
V's horse Anmer. The impact at ~35 mph was fatal..she never recovered

the support for the suffragettes extended throughout the country
confirmed by the crowds that lined the streets for her farewell
a well-organised occasion, crisp trappings worthy of a military funeral
her fearless zeal rose above personal concerns, a beacon of light
for all women to follow, in harmony with her message "Deeds, not words".

Neil Armstrong
How, when, where and...with whom...it all began.

An excerpt from President John Fitzgerald Kennedy's inaugural address on January 21st 1961, in which he clearly laid out his plan and priorities for himself, the United States of America and the world and then went on to say:

"All this will not be finished in the first one hundred days. Nor will it be finished in the first one thousand days, nor in the life of this Administration, nor even perhaps in our lifetime on this planet. But let us begin"

And this excerpt from his stirring speech at Rice University on September 12th 1962.

*We choose to go to the moon. We choose to go to the moon **in this decade** and do the other things, not because they are easy, but because they are hard, because that goal will serve to organize and measure the best of our energies and skills, because that challenge is one that we are willing to accept, one we are unwilling to postpone, and one which we intend to win, and the others, too."*

– President John Fitzgerald Kennedy

Neil Armstrong

(aka First Human Moonwalker)

The Boy

the dime stores in Ohio's little towns

is where young Neil got his model airplanes

of balsa wood that he modelled,

next tackled gasoline-powered prototypes

training his siblings to fling them

out the upstairs window so they would glide

and land further each time while

he recorded the spots where they landed

a proto-engineer at ten, he knew

what he wanted, mapping out his future

by obtaining his pilot's licence

on his sixteenth birthday

he was flying before he could drive.

The Test Pilot

a naval aviator in the Korean War,

then a degree in Aeronautical Engineering and

a test pilot for NASA. In his long career

flying more than two hundred different aircraft

gliders, jets, helicopters and studied

the X-15, a rocket-powered, missile shaped

aircraft that tested the limits of

high-altitude flight. While flying a Lunar Landing

Research Vehicle in May '68, to

simulate a lunar module's landings on the moon,

fuel for the attitude thrusters ran

low, and Armstrong was forced to eject unharmed,

just seconds before the LLRV crashed.

The First Human Moonwalker

Apollo 11's all-veteran crew members Neil

Armstrong, Michael Collins and Buzz Aldrin using
the command module, Columbia, with Neil

as Commander were blasted from earth, en-route
to the moon, approaching moon's orbit

Neil and Buzz now in the Lunar module, Eagle,
separated from Columbia to prepare for

the moon landing – while Collins was orbiting the
moon, waiting for Neil and Buzz to return.

Buzz is reported have seen Neil drop something
from his ppk* and lost in thought and

appeared to have been overcome by the immensity
of his feat, probably missing the daughter

he had lost to cancer at the age of two

"One small step for man ——a giant leap for mankind!"

ppk* = personal property kit

Marie Colvin

Henry Crabb Robinson, a reporter for the Times of London, was one of the earliest war correspondents when covering Napoleon's wars in Spain and Germany (1803-1815), as was William Hicks who chronicled the Battle of Trafalgar (1805) in the Times.

Prior to war correspondents, all news from frontlines was either banned or was heavily biased in favour of the nation that was responsible for the provocation and/or was the aggressor. Neutral observers were forbidden in theatres of war. It's only after the United Nations, a successor to the League of Nations, was formed in October 1945 that less biased and fairer reports of situations on the ground were being sent out to international news agencies.

Among the brave and upright war journalists, photographers and correspondents of the 20th and 21st centuries, the list includes stalwarts such as Fredrick Richard Dimbleby who was the first BBC war correspondent, Kate Adie, Martin Bell, Christiana Amanpour, Lindsey Hilsum, and the first famous American female photographer, Margaret Bourke-White.

War correspondents and investigative journalists have been the bane of corrupt governments ever since journalism and fair-minded news agencies began to oversee the behaviour and motives of warring nations. Often, the journalists have been deliberately targeted.

This is a poem about one of those brave souls, the intrepid British/American Marie Colvin, who selflessly placed her life on the line, every time she went onto the battlefield 'dying' to let her readers see and know what was actually happening on the ground.

Marie Colvin in Homs* City, Syria – 22 February 2012

"As I saw this baby die."

The nexus between corrupt governments and organised crime, is the reason
free speech is being strangled at birth. The targets of venom – mainly
investigative journalists, who train the spotlight on their despicable crimes.

Marie Colvin was one fearless woman pursuing the truth, tailing corrupt leaders
unafraid of their power. Her bravery was remarkable, integrity unquestionable,
dogged persistence in dangerous places would finally lead to her death.

Left eye blinded in the Sri Lankan Civil War, the blast of a rocket-propelled grenade,
instead of quitting she shrugged it off and carried on – with an eye-patch,
sending pics from frontlines so that you and I, could see with our unpatched eyes

our bloody world. The day before she was killed she saw a little boy struck by
a shrapnel piercing his chest, quoting *"his little tummy heaving and heaving*
to breathe, it was horrific, my heart broke, *as I saw this baby die"*. She insisted

'twas right to let the world see, the gruesome images of war, in pictures that show
the carnage they cannot or aren't allowed to see, as thousands of people have
to endure the ravages of 21st century savages, ruining the lives of citizens.

Authorities wanting to suppress news of their atrocities, targeted war reporters with
mortar bombs in Homs City* – striking her shelter – little did she know – within
hours of seeing that stricken baby die, she'd be lip-syncing – her final good-bye!

(Homs* = 3rd largest city of Syria after Aleppo in the north and Damascus in the south)

Rosa Parks

or

'twas a long way from Montgomery

no blacks allowed to use the front of the bus in Montgomery December 1,
1955 – but the daring defiance of Rosa Parks that day, to stand her ground
by sitting down, refusing to surrender her seat because of her colour – neither
budging nor grudging ridiculous threats of driver, de facto the mother of the Civil

Rights Movement – this single act of courage emboldened a race, to stand up
to the abomination of racism. Rosa was fined and arrested, reports said she
resisted because she was tired.. to quote her *"I was not tired, I was not old, I was*
only 42, No, the only tired I was, *was the tired of giving in."*

On February 1, 1960 at a whites-only lunch counter at Woolworths in North
Carolina, four black college students wouldn't stir until their coffee was
served...Of course it wasn't! – each time the police took them away, four others
just replaced them – nonviolent throughout the sit-ins kept spreading, TV pictures

of bread rolls, chips, ketchup and food used as missiles and when attacks on blacks
got physical, they stoically curled up on the floor, enduring gratuitous kicking -
no fear, not a tear..... no counter attack just passive resistance – such contrast of
courage and brute force on display, the movement was gaining the moral high

ground. Stalwarts Ralph Abernathy, Martin Luther King and others throughout
the fifties and sixties fought racism hard, King was shot dead dismantling
inequality, paving the way for whites with integrity to loathe the iniquity of
segregation – and blacks to realise their full potential – enter Barack Obama

Elected President of the United States!
November 4, 2008

Me Too

Despite the eleven-year hiatus when MeToo was first started by Tarana Burke in 2006 and Alyssa Milano setting off a viral awareness globally in 2018, it has now established itself as the firm overseer and arbiter of justice and protection for women who have been, and are in danger of being harmed by men in any way as a direct result of male misogynist behaviour.

MeToo – The unravelling of Harvestein

(aka dismantling patriarchy)

unbuttoned shirt, what awkward
awaiting prey, he praying the wait
snake smiling to himself

visceral grunts
will reward, the slimy
hoping to burst the

repressed squirt... of carnal,
spraying the object of the day
she is l'objet d'art – the one

lascivious, venal lust
who glides in ever hopeful
destined to get the part

while he, master bountiful bestows,
backs her onto the sprawling bed
shoving, this blubber of mankind,

nay thrusts himself and
– stupent protests, pushing,
aching to dislodge the

beached whale atop her... to no avail.
bulk of Harvestein there's nought to do
from the king and crown of tinseltown

Wedged 'tween bed and
but endure, humiliation
or it's curtains for career.

such power invested in strident
silence victims confronting them,
ownership replete with arrogance

men for generations helped
the audacious acts of
to boot..another wench...

Who gives a hoot?

Until..emboldened #MeToo's army
Moguls, the union of committed
heeding clarions to dismantle,

grew to strengths outstripping
sisters enjoined in battle
patriarchal citadels!

The Spanish Flu

The name "Spanish Flu" is grossly unfair to Spain because unlike the US, UK, France, Germany and Austria who were involved in World War 1 in 1918, neutral Spain did not keep secret all news about its influenza infections and deaths. Spain even admitted that their king, Alfonso XIII, had the infection. The countries at war had blocked all such news to keep the morale of their citizens high and to avoid encouraging the enemy. As a result, Spain was wrongly blamed as the originator of the pandemic which then dubiously became known as the Spanish Flu.

One remarkable lesson that could be learnt from the Spanish Flu of 1918-1919 was that this flu came in three waves – the second wave, the most lethal and the third being less lethal than the second but more than the first. The pandemic that we are witnessing today as I write this (11-06-2020) is still in its first wave with lockdown measures being eased throughout the world, even the scientists today can only hope there will not be a second wave.

Another oddity compared to the previous pandemics was that 99% of deaths in the US due to the Spanish Flu were of people under the age of 65 and half of them between 20 and 40 which is very unusual as previously they were aged 70 and over or babies under two years old.

Spanish Flu / La Grippe / Influenza" of 1918-1919

This deadly pandemic – frightening, lethal, indiscriminate, had little to do with Spain.
The wartime blackouts on news by countries to keep up morale, helped conceal its origin,
though evidence since recorded shows that it could have come from the US, or Chinese
labourers flown to Britain and France to free up locals for wartime duties.

US president Woodrow Wilson when signing the Treaty of Versaille, the British prime
minister David Lloyd George celebrating victory news, King Alfonso XIII of Spain, the
German Kaiser and Mahatma Gandhi all lucky to recover from this H1N1 virus strain
which was causing death and disruption throughout every corner of the world.

The Spanish Flu wiped out between 50 and 100 million people worldwide
in a single year, whereas World War 1, 'The Great War', from 1914 to 1918 had
killed 17 million in four...going further back, more than in the bubonic plague or Black
Death from 1347 to 1351 – and a flu rightly labelled the worst global disaster

The Forgotten Anniversary in 2018

It was the year of anniversaries   A century since women over thirty
could vote for the first time. It was   also the centenary of the end of the
First World War. Seventy years since   the formation of the State of Israel and
the NHS, and fifty years since the global   1968 revolts. Every one of them was
respectfully and rightfully commemorated.

But the most horrendous event that   had the greatest impact on humanity
in 1918, was forgotten completely   in its centenary year of 2018.
It's as though we didn't want to know   and deliberately turned our gaze away
from the Spanish Flu Pandemic. Laura   Spinney in "Pale Rider" said "*the flu
resculpted human populations more radically
than anything since the Black Death*"

Why did we forget or choose not to   remember, one answer perhaps is while
those celebrated and remembered,   were achievements with prizes, using
Spinney's words "*while wars have*   *victors, pandemics leave only the*
vanquished" …a protective shield   was the noise of the silence ———
enabling group therapy.. and recovery?

THE COVID-19 CAULDRON
Or
Never going back to the pre-coronavirus era

the stark warning of the virus from the
deliberately ignored by a secretive regime
would suffer. Human capacity to do evil
the custodians of this planet. Selfish streaks

Chinese ophthalmologist, Dr Li Wenliang,
despite knowing the devastation humanity
is the reason we cannot be trusted to be
inherent in our psyche neither shunned

nor shed until this COVID-19 cauldron we are
navels seeing the folly of running economies
towards the haves and have-lots, which was
as long it suited just those at the top......

in, calibrates our alchemy to gaze at our
and health services, immorally biased
blatantly obvious and tacitly approved for
until the shit hit the fan in Wuhan!

a rethink's essential, a world reimagined, lives
Pre-coronavirus era? It has gone forever......
focussed on fairer, compassionate, sharing
helpless getting timely support for humanity's

reset... never going back.......
the mindset and foresight now to be
of dwindling resources, the poorest and
sake... or becoming extinct

for creating these weakest links in the chain.

The rest, as we (are loath to) say – - is the present.

We're Livin' It!

Printed in Poland
by Amazon Fulfillment
Poland Sp. z o.o., Wrocław